RUSSIAN IMMIGRANTS

1860-1915

by Helen Frost

Content Consultant:
Natalie Batova, Director
Russian Cultural Centre, Washington, D.C.

Blue Earth Books

an imprint of Capstone Press
Mankato, Minnesota

Blue Earth Books are published by Capstone Press
151 Good Counsel Drive, P.O. Box 669, Mankato, Minnesota 56002
http://www.capstone-press.com

Library of Congress Cataloging-in-Publication Data
Frost, Helen, 1949-
    Russian immigrants, 1860–1915 / by Helen Frost.
    p. cm. — (Coming to America)
    Includes bibliographical references (p. 31) and index.
    Summary: Discusses the reasons Russian people left their homeland to come to America, the experiences the immigrants had in the new country, and the
    contributions this cultural group made to American society. Includes sidebars and activities.
    ISBN 0-7368-1209-1 (hardcover)
    1. Russian Americans—History—Juvenile literature. 2. Immigrants—United States—History—Juvenile literature. 3. United States—Emigration and
immigration—History—Juvenile literature. 4. Russia—Emigration and immigration—History—Juvenile literature. [1. Russian Americans—History
2. Immigrants—History. 3. United States—Emigration and immigration—History. 4. Russia—Emigration and immigration—History.] I. Title II. Coming
to America (Mankato, Minn.)
    E184.R9 F76 2003
    973' .049171—dc21   2001005948

Editorial credits
Editor: Katy Kudela
Series Designer: Heather Kindseth
Book Designer: Jennifer Schonborn
Photo Researcher: Stacy Foster
Product Planning Editor: Karen Risch

Photo credits
Bettmann/CORBIS, cover, 8, 9, 16; Gregg Andersen, flag images throughout; Scheufler Collection/CORBIS, 4; Hulton/Archive Photos, 7, 18, 20, 21; CORBIS, 10, 14; Capstone Press/Gary Sundermeyer, 11, 23; Minnesota Historical Society, 13; The State Russian Museum/CORBIS, 15; Vince Streano/CORBIS, 24, 26; Wolfgang Kaehler/CORBIS, 25; Mitchell Gerber/CORBIS, 29 (top); CinemaPhoto/CORBIS, 29 (bottom)

Special thanks to Chad Thompson, Irene Anders, and the children's library staff of the Allen County Public Library in Fort Wayne, Indiana, for assisting the author with research.

1 2 3 4 5 6 07 06 05 04 03 02

Contents

EARLY RUSSIAN IMMIGRANTS

Many women and children stayed in Russia while their husbands and fathers earned money in America.

S cientists believe that people began traveling between the United States and Russia 15,000 years ago. During the Ice Age, a narrow strip of dry land called the Bering Land Bridge connected Siberia and Alaska. Scientists believe that people walked across the land from Asia into North America. Over the course of thousands of years, some of their descendants probably migrated south into what is now the United States.

When the ice melted about 12,000 years ago, water covered the land bridge. The Bering Sea separated Russia and Alaska. During the 1700s, Russians sailed the short distance of 3.4 miles (5.5 kilometers) to Alaska.

Russian fur traders explored land inhabited by several groups of native Alaskans, including the Aleuts, Tlingits, Athabaskans, and Eskimos. In 1794, eight monks from a Russian monastery came to Alaska. They established the Russian Orthodox Mission to teach their religion, which is one of the many branches of Christianity.

In the 1700s, Alaska was not part of the United States. Russia claimed Alaska and sold it to the United States in 1867. At this time, about 800 Russians lived in Alaska. Many of them returned to Russia when Alaska became a U.S. territory. Some Russian men had married native Alaskan women and remained in Alaska with their families. Others moved to Russian settlements in California. The Russian Orthodox Mission also moved to California. It later established headquarters in New York.

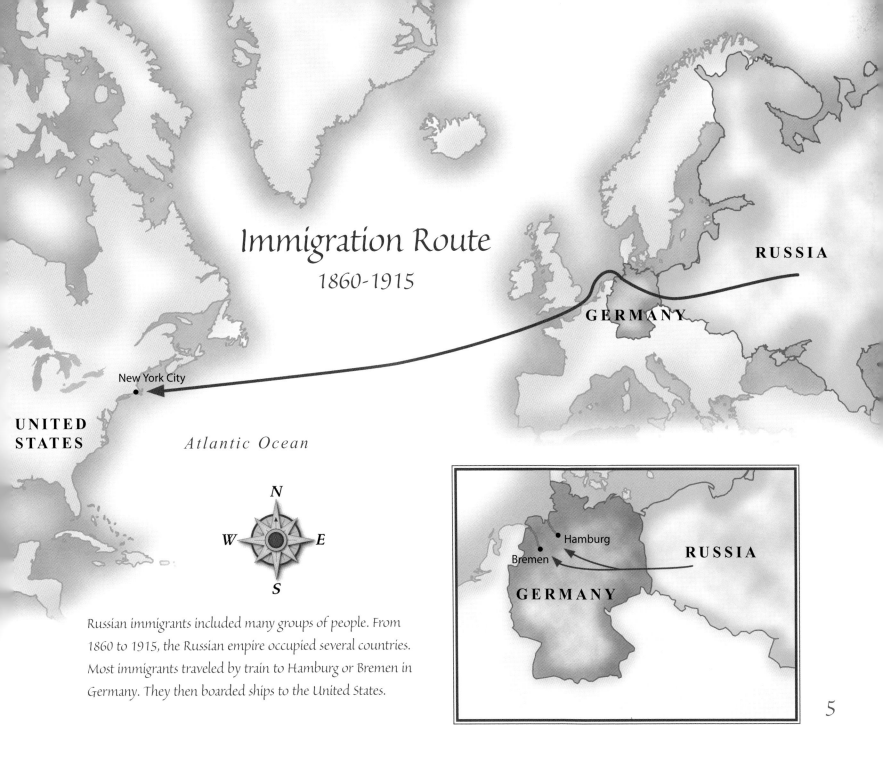

Immigration Route
1860-1915

RUSSIA

GERMANY

New York City

UNITED
STATES

Atlantic Ocean

N
W   E
S

Russian immigrants included many groups of people. From 1860 to 1915, the Russian empire occupied several countries. Most immigrants traveled by train to Hamburg or Bremen in Germany. They then boarded ships to the United States.

Hamburg

Bremen

RUSSIA

GERMANY

Russian Words in Alaskan Native Languages

In 1741, Russian explorer Vitus Bering and his crew arrived in Kayak Island, Alaska. Russian fur traders soon began exploring the new land. In 1794, monks from the Russian Orthodox Church founded a mission in Kodiak, Alaska. The Russians brought with them their language, traditions, and customs. The influence of the Russian explorers, fur traders, and missionaries in Alaska can be seen in these words that are now part of Native Alaskan languages.

English	Russian	Yupik Eskimo	Koyukon
butter	máslo (MAHS-loh)	masslaq (MAH-slak)	baasdle (BAS-dluh)
hammer	molotók (mahlah-TOK)	mulut'uuk (MOO-LOO-TOOK)	maalaadok (MA-LA-DOHK)
soap	m'ylo (MEE-loh)	miilaq (MEE-lahk)	meele (MEE-luh)
table	stol (STOHL)	stuuluq (STOO-LOOK)	sdole (STO-luh)
teapot	cháynik (CHAY-nik)	caanik (CHAH-NIK)	tsaayneek (TSEYE-NECK)

During the 1800s, people began to emigrate from the western part of Russia to the eastern part of America. By 1920, the total number of Russian immigrants in America was reported at 3,280,249.

These immigrants included many different groups of people. Between 1860 and 1915, the boundaries between Russia and neighboring countries frequently changed. Poland, Finland, Estonia, Latvia, Lithuania, Ukraine, and several other countries were sometimes part of the Russian empire. People often traveled from one country to another within Europe. They stayed awhile, and then moved again.

Two main waves of Russian immigrants came to America between 1860 and 1920. Before 1914, most immigrants were peasants who had little money or education. They planned to return to Russia to buy land with the money they earned in America. More than half of these immigrants returned to Russia.

In 1914, Russia entered World War I (1914–1918). Russia suffered from economic troubles and food shortages. In 1917, the people of Russia overthrew Tsar Nicholas II, the ruler of Russia. This revolution ended the tsarist rule in Russia.

Around that time, a second group of emigrants left from Russia. This group was smaller, and they generally were wealthier and more educated than those who had left Russia before 1914.

Many immigrants arrived in America with few possessions. Immigrants were often very tired after the long journey.

LIFE IN THE OLD COUNTRY

Russian peasants enjoyed listening to music. They often played balalaikas, three-stringed musical instruments.

Russia is the largest country in the world, stretching across the northern part of Europe and Asia. Russia's land includes forests, mountains, and plains, as well as rivers, lakes, and oceans. In much of Russia, the winters are long and cold, while the summers are warm and short. The growing season is just a few months long. People in Russia must grow enough food in a short time to last through the long winter.

For hundreds of years, a series of powerful leaders called tsars ruled Russia. Peasant farmers did not own their own land. Instead, they worked for wealthy landowners who did not pay them for their work. The peasants had to give a large share of the food they grew to their landowner. This system made it difficult for them to feed their large families. Children worked in the fields along with their parents. Most children did not go to school and never learned to read.

In the late 1800s, about 85 percent of Russians were peasant farmers. They lived in small houses with thatched roofs made of straw. They made soup with potatoes and other vegetables. Rye bread and beet soup, called borscht, was a common Russian meal.

During the long winter, animals stayed in houses with the people. People kept horses to work in the fields, and they raised cows for milk. But they seldom could afford to raise animals for meat.

Russian peasants worked many hours in the fields.

Russian peasants spent most of their time working in the fields. After the fieldwork, Russians enjoyed spending time with their families. During long winter evenings, they played flutes and balalaikas, three-stringed musical instruments. They also enjoyed singing, dancing, and storytelling. Women embroidered by stitching colorful designs onto clothing.

From 1547 to 1861, the tsars did not allow the peasants to move about the country. Peasants lived and worked in the same place all their lives. During this time, the peasants were called serfs.

In 1861, Tsar Alexander II freed all Russian serfs, so they then could move to other areas. The tsar also gave peasants the opportunity to buy land. The plots were

Many Jews emigrated from Russia during the early 1900s.

In 1891, and again in 1909, bad weather ruined the grain crops in Russia. Many people faced starvation. Some people moved to Russian cities to work in factories. Others left Russia to look for work in other countries, including the United States.

Russians who went to the United States to work often returned to Russia. They saved the money they earned from working in factories and returned home. Some of those who stayed in the United States wrote back to their friends and relatives, encouraging them to come to America.

The government punished people who did not follow the practices and beliefs of the Russian Orthodox Church. Russian Jews suffered greatly during the late 1800s and early 1900s. Many died in "pogroms," which were attacks on Jewish communities. Several groups of Russians, including Russian Jews, came to America to seek religious freedom.

In 1917, a group of Russians, called Bolsheviks, challenged the rules of the tsar. They did not like the system that allowed a few landowners to profit from the work of many peasant farmers. The Bolsheviks, under the leadership of Vladimir Lenin, took charge of the government and seized the land and businesses.

Many people whose property had been seized by the Bolsheviks fled to America. Most of the Russians who came to America after 1917 were skilled workers or people who had been officers in the tsarist army.

often expensive. Some free land was available to the peasants, but these plots of land were very small.

Many peasants accepted the free plots because they could not afford to buy larger areas of land. But the land was seldom enough to make a living. Many families ran out of food and supplies before the winter season ended.

Medovnichki (Honey Cookies)

Peasants often used honey in place of sugar to sweeten their recipes. Honey was inexpensive and is the main ingredient of the traditional Russian cookie Medovnichki (mi-DOV-nich-kee). Russians enjoyed these honey cookies with tea, their favorite drink.

What You Need

Ingredients
nonstick cooking spray
1 cup (250 mL) softened butter
1 egg
2 cups (500 mL) honey
4 $\frac{1}{2}$ cups (1 liter and 125 mL) flour
$\frac{1}{2}$ teaspoon (2 mL) baking soda
1 teaspoon (5 mL) cinnamon
1 $\frac{1}{2}$ (375 mL) cups chopped walnuts
   or hazelnuts

Equipment
baking sheet
two medium mixing bowls
dry-ingredient measuring cups
electric mixer
measuring spoons
sifter
plastic wrap
pot holders
wire cooling racks
metal spatula

What You Do

1. Grease the baking sheet with nonstick cooking spray. Set aside.

2. Put the butter in a mixing bowl. With an electric mixer, beat the butter on medium speed until it is fluffy.

3. Add the egg and honey and beat the mixture again until it is creamy.

4. Sift the flour, baking soda, and cinnamon together in the second mixing bowl.

5. Add the sifted dry ingredients to the creamy mixture, half a cup at a time. Mix well after each addition.

6. Stir the chopped nuts into the dough.

7. Cover the bowl with plastic wrap. Chill the dough in the refrigerator for at least one hour.

8. Preheat oven to 350°F (180°C).

9. Form the dough into balls about the size of a walnut. Place the dough balls on the prepared baking sheet about 2 inches (5 centimeters) apart.

10. Place the baking sheet in oven. Bake at 350°F (180°C) for 15 minutes.

11. Remove cookies from baking sheet with metal spatula and place onto a wire cooling rack.

Makes about 6 dozen cookies

11

THE TRIP OVER

"Mostly we ate hard-boiled eggs, raw potatoes, and we got an occasional apple. I don't remember a dining room or anything. It was just a mass of people. And whatever you wore, and whatever you had, was with you. We didn't have any luggage or anything like that."

—Betty Garoff, born 1913, emigrated from Russia in 1921 at age 8

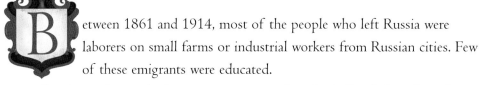

Between 1861 and 1914, most of the people who left Russia were laborers on small farms or industrial workers from Russian cities. Few of these emigrants were educated.

Russian emigrants had to overcome many obstacles before being allowed to leave Russia. Emigrants had to pay a fee to apply for a passport. They then paid another fee to receive their passports. Most people did not have enough money to pay these fees. Many people did not know how to read the application or write well enough to answer the questions on the form.

Most emigrants saved for years to have enough money for the trip. People needed money for their ship tickets, food, and expenses on the way. They also needed money to get started in America. Many Russian families could save enough money to send only one person, usually a son, to America. When he settled and began working, the son would send money home. His parents used this money to buy land in Russia or to send another family member to America.

In 1910, there were about 137 Russian men for every 100 Russian women who immigrated to America. Some Russian women traveled alone. Other women went

Russian husbands and sons often came to America before other family members. Saving money for a steamship ticket to America took a long time.

13

Most Russian immigrants could afford tickets only in the steerage section.
Conditions in the steerage section were crowded and unpleasant.

with their husbands or with their parents. Some women left Russia to avoid marrying a husband their parents chose for them. Others immigrated to the United States looking for a new, exciting experience.

When Russians left their country, they could take very little with them. They usually packed only one trunk or suitcase, with a few clothes and precious possessions. They took silverware, tools, Bibles, and photographs. They also took special items such as goose down comforters and hand-embroidered clothing.

Many Russian emigrants started their trip by walking or riding in a hay wagon to a railway station in a nearby city. They then traveled to the Russian border. Most Russians crossed the border into Germany and took another train to the port cities of Hamburg or Bremen. From Germany, steamships carried passengers to America.

The agents who sold tickets on the steamships sometimes refused to sell ship tickets to weak or sick passengers. Unhealthy immigrants often were not accepted into America. If an immigrant was turned away, the shipping company had to provide free transportation back to the port where the person had boarded. The agents rejected about five out of every 100 Russians who tried to buy tickets.

The trip from Germany to America took two to three weeks. Most Russian immigrants traveled in the steerage section of the ships because it was the least expensive.

Embroidered items were some of the few possessions Russian immigrants brought with them. This colorful towel dates to the early 1800s. The image on the towel is the firebird, a traditional fairy tale character.

Steerage was a section that held up to 2,000 passengers in the lowest part of the ship. Steerage conditions were uncomfortable and crowded. Passengers slept in hammocks, or in bunks stacked three beds high. Steerage had three sections—one for men, one for women, and another for families. This section of the steamship offered very little privacy.

ARRIVING IN AMERICA

About 70 percent of Russian immigrants entered the United States in New York City. Others arrived in Philadelphia and other eastern cities in the United States. As soon as they arrived in America, immigrants passed through an immigration checkpoint. Inspectors decided who could stay in America.

From 1820 to 1892, immigrants arriving in New York City passed through the Castle Garden immigration

station. Castle Garden soon became too small to accommodate the increasing number of new immigrants. In 1892, a new immigration station opened near the Statue of Liberty. Ellis Island became the arrival point for thousands of immigrants who came to America.

A total of 750,000 Russian immigrants passed through Ellis Island between 1892 and 1924. During those busy years of immigration at Ellis Island, up to 10,000 immigrants arrived each day.

Officials at Ellis Island could not always keep up with the arriving immigrants. Passengers sometimes had to wait on the steamships for several days before a boat took them to the immigration station. They sometimes had to wait again on these crowded transport boats.

When the immigrants did get to Ellis Island, they often waited in long lines for several hours before meeting the inspection officials. Medical officials checked immigrants for diseases. The officials made chalk marks on immigrants' clothing to indicate any medical problems. The letter "L" indicated an immigrant was lame and had difficulty walking. The letter "X" suggested a mental illness. About 20 percent of arriving immigrants received a chalk mark. A doctor inspected these people and decided if they could be treated and allowed entry into the country.

After the medical inspection, immigrants had to pass a legal inspection. Inspectors asked the immigrants questions to determine whether they would be good citizens or not. Inspectors also wanted to be sure immigrants were able to support themselves in America. Inspectors asked questions such as: "Do you have any money?" "What was your occupation in Russia?" "Is someone meeting you?"

The immigrants who passed the medical and legal inspections entered the United States. Officials held the others for further observation or questioning at

Immigrants arriving at Ellis Island spent most of their time waiting in lines. Ellis Island officials saw up to 10,000 immigrants each day. Russian immigrants were just one of the many ethnic groups that immigrated to the United States during the late 1800s and early 1900s.

Ellis Island. About 2 percent of the immigrants were sent back to their home country. Most of the immigrants who failed the medical inspections stayed in the hospital until they got better.

Many Russian immigrants stayed in the port cities where they arrived. They found jobs working in steel mills, meat packing plants, and the garment industry.

Russian immigrants arriving in the early 1800s had to find their way around with very little help. As more and more Russians settled in the United States, it became easier for immigrants to begin their new life in America. By the late 1800s, most new immigrants knew someone already living in America. Russian Americans who had been in the United States for a few years organized immigrant aid societies to help new arrivals.

Many immigrants traveled by train to other states including Pennsylvania and Illinois. For those who did not speak English, a translator was ready to help find the correct train. The translator pinned tags onto immigrants' clothing so the train conductors would know where the immigrants were going.

"Everybody had something to give me for help. It wasn't a question of money, it was a question of being a human being to a human being. And in those days people were apparently that way. There were so many nice people that were trying to help us when we came to this country."

—Clara Larsen,
a Russian Jewish immigrant in 1908

Many factory jobs were available in the United States. Russian immigrants worked in steel mills, meat packing plants, coal mines, and the garment industry. Many children also took jobs to help their families earn money.

SURVIVING IN AMERICA

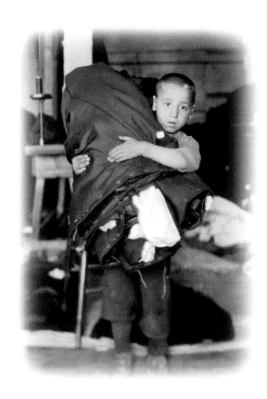

Children worked in factories to help earn money for their families.

ost Russian immigrants who came to America before World War I arrived with little or no money. They needed to start working right away, so they took whatever jobs they could find.

Often Russian immigrants first worked in industrial factories in the port cities where they arrived. Many immigrants found jobs in coal mines and steel mills in Pennsylvania and Illinois.

In New York and other large cities, many Russian immigrants worked in the garment industry. Garment factories were crowded with people sewing clothes. The workrooms got the nickname "sweatshops" because they were poorly aired and became very hot. Russian immigrants worked 10 to 14 hours a day, six or even seven days a week, and earned $5 to $6 a week.

Russian immigrants took additional jobs to earn more money. Many immigrants took home piecework. Immigrants received a small amount of money for each piece of clothing they sewed.

Children often worked the same hours as adults, trying to earn money for their families. They worked many hours in dirty and dangerous conditions. Children often suffered from illness and exhaustion due to poor working conditions.

In large cities, Russian immigrant families often lived in small apartments in buildings called tenements. Even though the apartments were crowded, families sometimes shared one or more of their rooms with other immigrants to save money.

Families sometimes shared their rooms with other immigrants to save money. Conditions in the tenement buildings were crowded. Immigrants often shared their meals together in a single dining room.

Unmarried women immigrants from Russia often ran boardinghouses as a way of supporting themselves. Single men and women, and men whose families were still in Russia, lived in these boardinghouses.

Many Russian immigrants, including boys as young as 8 years old, worked in coal mines. The work was hot, dirty, tiring, and dangerous. Many immigrants suffered from lung disease later in life from inhaling coal dust in the mines.

Coal miners often lived near the coal mines in shanty towns. The houses in shanty towns were small shacks with little heat and no plumbing.

21

Russian Americans worked to improve working conditions for themselves and others. They organized strikes, refusing to work until their working conditions improved. Russian Americans also started labor unions. This organized group of workers fought for better working conditions. Labor unions forced employers to shorten working days, give lunch breaks, and pay workers a fair wage.

During the early 1900s, labor unions also stopped employers from hiring children. Union members believed children should be in school learning and planning for their future. In some cases, this law was a hardship because families needed the extra income. But the immigrants knew it was important for children to go to school.

Many Russian Americans knew several languages because people of so many nations had been part of Russia at various times in history. The Russian Americans could speak to immigrants from other countries and encourage them to join unions. The Russian immigrants' skill in labor organizing was an advantage.

But after the 1917 revolution in Russia, many things changed. In 1922, Russia and several other countries united to form the Union of Soviet Socialist Republics (USSR). A communist government came into power. The government took land, houses, and factories away from individuals. Government officials gave out work assignments and workers shared in the profits of the government-run companies.

Many Americans did not like the idea of communism. They were worried that Russian Americans would start a revolution in the United States. This concern was called the "Red Scare." In the winter of 1919–1920, United States officials arrested thousands of Russian Americans who had expressed ideas that officials considered too severe. They sent about 245 of these Russian Americans back to Russia.

★ Dyeing Eggs with Onion Skins ★

Dyeing Easter eggs is a tradition in the Russian Orthodox Church. The Easter egg is an Orthodox symbol of eternal life. Russians continued this tradition when they came to America. Russian immigrants arrived in the United States with very little money. Despite their poor conditions, they found ways to follow their traditions. Before the Easter season began, Russian Americans saved onion skins. Russian Americans used onion skins to dye Easter eggs. These colored eggs were then put into baskets with other traditional foods and brought to church. After the food was blessed, people took the food home for an Easter feast.

What You Need

outer skins from 20 to 30 onions

six (or more) white eggs

enough water to cover the eggs

pan

stove

spoon

What You Do

1. Start collecting onion skins several months before coloring the eggs. Save the dry outer onion skins in a paper bag or other container. More onion skins make darker colors on the eggs.

2. Put the onion skins into the pan.

3. Place the eggs on top of the onion skins, being careful not to break or crack the eggs.

4. Cover the eggs and onion skins with water.

5. Put the pan on a burner on the stove.

6. With adult supervision, bring the water in the pan to a boil over medium heat.

7. Continue cooking the eggs for 15 minutes, gently stirring the eggs and onion skins every few minutes.

8. Remove the pan from the heat and use the spoon to lift the colored eggs out of the water. The colored eggs will be hard-boiled and should be stored in the refrigerator.

9. Use the eggs as decorations or serve them to eat.

KEEPING TRADITIONS

Today, Russian American communities thrive in many cities in America. Some of the largest Russian American communities are found in New York City, Los Angeles, Chicago, and Philadelphia.

In these communities, Russian Orthodox churches often play an important role. Easter is an especially important holiday. Women prepare paskha, a cheesecake. They also make a fruit and nut bread called kulich. They then fill baskets with paskha, kulich, and colored eggs, sometimes dyed with onion skins. They bring the baskets to church on the Thursday before Easter, where a priest blesses the food.

Communities of Old Believers in Oregon and Alaska continue the traditions of their Russian ancestors. The Old Believers were one of several religious groups that came to America during the 1800s to seek religious freedom.

Today, the communities of Old Believers continue to speak Russian and wear clothes similar to those worn by people in Russia during the 1600s. Men and boys wear a long-sleeved Russian shirt called a rubashka, secured with a belt. Women and girls wear a rubashka under a jumper called a sarafan.

The influence of Russian traditions in Alaska is still evident in the names of many Alaskan people and places. Some Alaskan communities feature Russian names

Traditional Russian clothing worn by women and girls includes a long-sleeved shirt called a rubashka. It is worn under a jumper called a sarafan.

Many Russian Americans continue to follow the teachings of the Russian Orthodox Church.

Specialty stores in Alaska feature Russian artwork and crafts. This woman is looking at a matryoshka, a Russian nesting doll.

including Sitka, Nikolai, Ivanof Bay, and Golovin. Russian Orthodox churches are part of many Alaskan communities.

Russian Americans continue to keep a close connection with their Russian heritage. In recent years, Russian Americans have created web sites to share news and information about cultural events, business opportunities, and history. Russian American publications, such as *Russian Life*, also keep Russian Americans updated and informed.

Many Russian Americans have made important contributions to the United States in various fields. In science, George Gamow wrote and taught about the origin of the universe. In politics, Bella Abzug was a U.S. Congresswoman who worked for health care and civil rights during the 1970s. In economics, Wassily Leontief won the 1973 Nobel Prize for world economics.

Other Russian Americans have made notable contributions in the arts. Igor Stravinsky was a well-known composer whose works included the two ballets *The Firebird* and *The Rite of Spring*. Vladimir Horowitz was a famous pianist. George Balanchine established the New York City Ballet in 1948.

Today, more than 2 million Americans identify themselves as having Russian ancestry. People continue to celebrate Russian traditions throughout the United States. Many Russian Americans celebrate Maslenitsa at the end of February. This weeklong holiday celebrates the end of winter. Russian Americans celebrate Maslenitsa with traditional songs, dances, games, and food. Pancakes are the traditional Maslenitsa food because they represent the spring sun.

★ Make a Family Tree ★

Genealogy is the study of family history. Genealogists often record this history in the form of a family tree. This chart records a person's ancestors, such as parents, grandparents, and great-grandparents.

Start your own family tree with the names of your parents and grandparents. Ask family members for their full names, including their middle names. Remember that your mother and grandmothers likely had a different last name before they were married. This name, called a maiden name, probably is the same as their fathers' last name.

Making a family tree helps you to know your ancestors and the countries from which they emigrated. Some people include the dates and places of birth with each name on their family tree. Knowing when and where these relatives were born will help you understand from which immigrant groups you have descended.

There are many ways to find information for your family tree. Ask for information from your parents, grandparents, and as many other older members of your family as you can. Some people research official birth and death records to find the full names of relatives. Genealogical societies often have information that will help with family tree research. If you know the cemetery where family members are buried, you may find some of the information you need on the gravestones.

Your father's mother

Your mother's father

Your father's father

Your mother's mother

Your father

Your mother

You

★ TIMELINE ★

1700

1794
The Russian Orthodox Mission settles in Kodiak, Alaska.

1741
Russian explorer Vitus Bering and his crew land their boat on Kayak Island, Alaska.

1800

1861
Tsar Alexander II grants freedom to Russian serfs. They can move to other areas if they desire.

1867
The United States purchases Alaska from Russia for 7.2 million dollars.

1891
Bad weather ruins grain crops in Russia.

1892
Ellis Island Immigration Station opens.

1900

1909
Bad weather ruins grain crops in Russia.

1901–1910
Decade of great emigration from Russia; 1,597,306 people leave Russia.

1914–1918
Russia enters World War I.

1917
Revolution begins in Russia.

1920
The total number of Russian immigrants in America reported to be 3,280,249.

1922
USSR is formed.

1918
Waves of educated and wealthy property owners begin to arrive in the United States after the Russian Revolution.

Bella Abzug (1920–1998) Born to Russian immigrants, Abzug worked for social justice all her life. She served in the U.S. Congress from 1971–1977. In 1991, she organized an international conference on women and the environment.

Isaac Asimov (1920–1992) Born in Russia, Asimov came to the United States with his parents in 1923. He wrote more than 470 books on many subjects including science, history, and literature. He is best known as a science fiction writer.

Mikhail Baryshnikov (1948–) Born to Russian parents in Riga, Latvia, Baryshnikov won great recognition in Russia as a classical ballet dancer. As a young man, he first moved to Canada and later to the United States, becoming a United States citizen in 1986. He is the artistic director of the American Ballet Theater.

Michael Douglas

Michael Douglas (1944–) Douglas was born in New Brunswick, New Jersey. He is the son of actor Kirk Douglas, whose parents were Russian immigrants. Like his father, Douglas became an actor. In recent years, he has worked as a movie producer and director.

Igor Sikorsky (1889–1972) Born and educated in Russia, Sikorsky immigrated to New York in 1919. He designed airplanes. In 1939, he designed and built the world's first helicopter.

Natalie Wood (1938–1983) Wood was born Natasha Gurdin in San Francisco, California. She began acting at the age of 4. She appeared in many films including *Miracle on 34th Street*, *Rebel Without a Cause*, and *West Side Story*.

Natalie Wood

Words to Know

ancestor (AN-sess-tur)—a member of one's family who lived a long time ago

balalaika (BAL-uh-LI-kuh)—a three-stringed Russian instrument with a triangular body and long neck

descendant (di-SEND-uhnt)—a person's child and the generations of a family born after that child

embroider (em-BROI-dur)—to sew a picture or a design onto cloth

emigrate (EM-uh-grate)—to leave your own country in order to live in another one

immigrant (IM-uh-gruhnt)—someone who comes from another country to live permanently in a new one

port (PORT)—a harbor or place where boats and ships can dock or anchor safely

revolution (rev-uh-LOO-shun)—an uprising by the people of a country that attempts to change its system of government; the Bolsheviks led the 1917 revolution in Russia.

Siberia (si-BIHR-ee-uh)—a large region of Asian Russia; Siberia has very long and cold winters.

steamship (STEEM-ship)—a boat powered by steam; most Russian immigrants came to America on steamships.

steerage (STIHR-age)—the lower section of a passenger ship with accommodations for passengers who paid the lowest fares

tenement (TEN-uh-muhnt)—a three- or four-story building designed to house eight to 10 families

tsar (ZAR)—an emperor of Russia before the revolution of 1917

To Learn More

Gray, Susan Heinrichs. *Russia*. First Reports. Minneapolis, Minn.: Compass Point Books, 2002.

Greene, Meg. *The Russian-Americans*. Immigrants in America. San Diego, Calif.: Lucent Books, 2002.

Nickles, Greg. *Russia: The Culture*. The Lands, Peoples and Cultures Series. New York: Crabtree Publishing Company, 2000.

Rebman, Renee, C. *Life on Ellis Island*. The Way People Live. San Diego, Calif.: Lucent Books, 2000.

Strickler, Jim. *Russia of the Tsars*. World History Series. San Diego, Calif.: Lucent Books, 1998.

Places to Write and Visit

The Balch Institute for Ethnic Studies
18 South Seventh Street
Philadelphia, PA 19106

Ellis Island Library
Statue of Liberty National Monument
Liberty Island
New York, NY 10004

Russian Center of San Francisco
2450 Sutter Street
San Francisco, CA 94115

Russian Cultural Centre
1825 Phelps Place, NW
Washington, DC 20008

United States Immigration and Naturalization Service Historian
425 I Street NW, Room CAB-1100
Washington, DC 20536

Internet Sites

The Balch Institute for Ethnic Studies
http://www.balchinstitute.org

Ellis Island
http://powayusd.sdcoe.k12.ca.us/usonline/worddoc/
ellisislandsite.htm

Fort Ross State Historic Park
http://www.mcn.org/1/rrparks/fortross/

My History is America's History – Kids' Corner
http://www.myhistory.org/kids/index.html

The Lower Eastside Tenement Museum – Virtual Tour
http://www.tenement.org/index_virtual.html

Russian Center of San Francisco
http://www.russiancentersf.com

Index